七步诗
The Seven Step Poem

ADAPTED, TRANSLATED, AND ILLUSTRATED BY

Wyatt To

LUMINARE PRESS

WWW.LUMINAREPRESS.COM

七步诗

The Seven Step Poem

Copyright © 2024 by Wyatt To

Printed in the United States of America

Luminare Press
442 Charnelton St.
Eugene, OR 97401
www.luminarepress.com

LCCN: 2024901249
ISBN: 979-8-88679-482-3

送给妈妈，因为她为我付中文课的学费。

To my mom, who paid for my Chinese lessons.

xiǎo péng yǒu　　nǐ men yǒu mei yǒu xiōng dì　hái shì jiě mèi ma　　nǐ men yǒu shí hou huì

小朋友，你们有没有兄弟还是姐妹吗？你们有时候会

bu huì gēn tā menchǎo jià　　zhōng guó lì shǐ shàng yǒu yí gè zhù míng de gù shì　　zhè ge

不会跟他们吵架？中国历史上有一个著名的故事。这个

gù shì lǐ shì guān yú yí gè gē gē jí dù tā dì dì de cái huá　　gù yì gěi tā

故事里是关于一个哥哥嫉妒他弟弟的才华，故意给他

yí jiàn zuò bù dào de shì

一件做不到的事。

Hey kids, do you have any siblings? Do you sometimes argue with them? In Chinese history, there is a famous story. This story is about an older brother's jealousy of his younger brother's skill, and how the older brother would purposefully give his sibling an impossible task.

sān guó shí qī wèi guó de huáng dì cáo cāo yǒu hǎo duō gè hái zi   kě shì tā zuì xǐ huan
三国时期魏国的 皇帝曹操有好多个孩子，可是他最喜欢

de shì tā dì sān gè ér zǐ   cáo zhí hé dì èr ér zǐ cáo pī
的是他第三个儿子，曹植和第二儿子曹丕。

During the War of the Three States, the Emperor of the Wei,
Cao Wei, had many children, but his favorites were his third
son Cao Zhi and second son Cao Pi.

曹植
Cao Zhi

曹丕
Cao Pi

cáo zhí shì cáo pī de dì dì　　rén men dōu ài tā　　yīn wéi chú le tā hěn cōngmíng
曹植是曹丕的弟弟。人们都爱他，因为除了他很聪明

yǐ wài　　yě hěn yǒu cái huá　　yóu qí shì tā xiě de shī yòu shēn yòu měi　　néng gòu
以外，也很有才华。尤其是他写的诗又深又美，能够

gǎndòng rénxīn　　kěshì　　zuì zhòngyào de shì　　tā shì yígè　　xīndìshànliáng de
感动人心。可是，最重要的是，他是一个心地善良的

hǎorén　　tā yě　　lèyú　　zhù rén
好人。他也乐于助人。

Cao Zhi was the little brother of Cao Pi. Everybody loved him because not only was he smart, but he was also incredibly skilled. Particularly, his written poems were deep, beautiful, and able to move the hearts of others. However, what was most important about him was that he was a kind person. He enjoyed helping others.

曹丕是曹植的哥哥。人们都怕他，因为除了他狡猾的个性以外，他也很残暴。

cáo pī shì cáo zhí de gēgē　rénmen dōu pà tā　yīnwéi chúle tā jiǎohuá de gèxìng yǐwài tā yě hěn cánbào

Cao Pi was the older brother of Cao Zhi. Everybody feared him because not only was he cunning, but he was also cruel.

cáo pī wúlùn zuò shī huò xiě wénzhāng dōu méiyǒu tā dìdì de hǎo suǒyǐ
曹丕无论作诗或写文章都没有他弟弟的好，所以
tā zǒngshì jídù tā dìdì de cáihuá　　tā shì gè huài xīn rén
他总是嫉妒他弟弟的才华。他是个坏心人。

Cao Pi could not write poems as well as Cao Zhi, and
so he always was jealous of his little brother's talent.
He was a bad hearted person.

cáocāo　yǐqián　xiǎngràng cáo zhí dāng huángdì　　dànshì　juéde　tā　xīndì　tài shànliáng

曹操以前想让曹植当皇帝，但是觉得他心地太善良。

cáocāo　dānxīn　rúguǒ　ràng cáo zhí dāng huángdì dehuà　　tā huì　guǎnlǐ　bù liǎo guó jiā

曹操担心如果让曹植当皇帝的话，他会管理不了国家。

yú shì　　tā jiù xuǎn cáo pī dāng le huáng dì

于是，他就选曹丕当了皇帝。

Cao Wei initially had planned for Cao Zhi to become emperor, but felt that he would be too soft-hearted. Cao Wei worried if Cao Zhi did become emperor, he would be unable to govern properly. And so instead, Cao Wei had Cao Pi become emperor.

cáo pī dāng le huáng dì yǐ hòu　　tā hái shì jí dù cáo zhí de cái néng

曹丕当了皇帝以后，他还是嫉妒曹植的才能。

When Cao Pi became emperor, he still was jealous of Cao Zhi's talent.

cáo pī zhīdào dào dàjiā dōu xǐhuan tā dìdì ér bù xǐhuan tā yīn cǐ tā jiù
曹丕知道到大家都喜欢他弟弟而不喜欢他，因此他就
xiǎngzhǎo dào yí gè jī huì shāng hài tā
想找到一个机会伤害他。

Cao Pi knew that everybody liked his little brother and not him, and so Cao Pi tried to think of ways to hurt him.

有一天，曹丕终于找到一个借口伤害他。

One day, Cao Pi finally thought of an excuse to hurt him.

tā zhào jí le suǒ yǒu de rén zài dà jiā de miànqián duì cáo zhí shuō
他召集了所有的人，在大家的面前对曹植说：

He gathered a crowd, and in front of everyone he said to Cao Zhi:

nǐ zhī cuò le ma
"你知错了吗？"

"Do you know what you did wrong?"

cáo zhí yǐjīng zhīdào tā gēgē jídù tā de cáihuá yìzhí zài zhǎo jīhuì shānghài
曹植已经知道他哥哥嫉妒他的才华，一直在找机会伤害

tā suǒyǐ tā méi huídá
他，所以他没回答。

Cao Zhi knew that his brother was jealous of his ability, and that Cao Pi had been looking for an opportunity to hurt him. He did not say anything.

曹丕大笑着说，"你不说话就表是你承认了！依照我们国家的法律，你应该被判死刑。但是，因为你是我的弟弟，所以我会给你一个活命的机会。"

Cao Pi laughed and cried, "Your silence is proof of your acknowledgement! By the laws of our state, you should face the death penalty. However, because you and I are brothers, I am willing to give you an opportunity to save yourself."

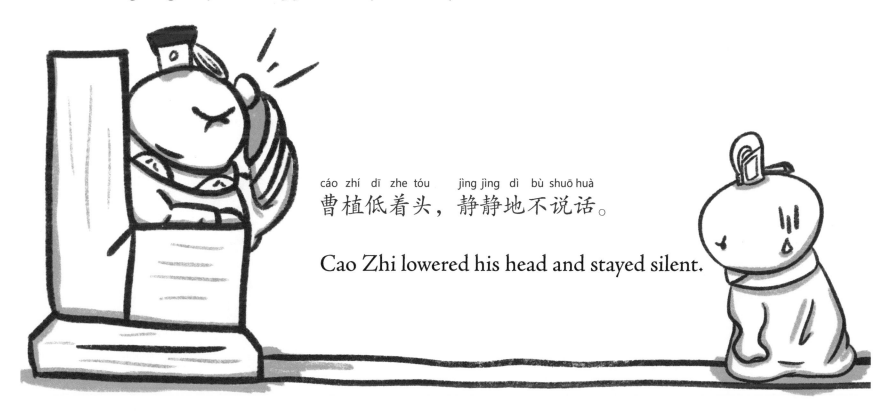

曹植低着头，静静地不说话。

Cao Zhi lowered his head and stayed silent.

曹丕得意地接着说，"听说你写的诗特别感人。

Cao Pi, full of himself, said, "They say your poems are excellent at moving people.

^{nà xiànzài wǒ yào nǐ zài qī bù zhīnèi xiǎng chū lái yī shǒu dòng rén de hǎo shī}
那现在我要你在七步之内想出来一首动人的好诗，
^{zuò bù dào de huà wǒ jiù bǎ nǐ sòng qù sǐ láo}
做不到的话，我就把你送去死牢。"

Right now, I want you to walk seven steps and come up
with a fantastic poem by the end of them. If you can't, then
I will have you killed."

^{shuō wán liǎo yǐ hòu cáo pī dé yì dì hā hā dà xiào}
说完了以后，曹丕得意地哈哈大笑。

Once he finished talking, Cao Pi let out
a big laugh.

cáo zhí míng bái gē gē de xīn jī　jué de shāng xīn jí le　suī rán zhè ge tiǎo zhàn duì cáo
曹植明白哥哥的心机，觉得伤心极了。虽然这个挑战对曹

zhí yì diǎn er gōng dào dōu méi yǒu　dàn shì tā xiǎng bù chū qí tā de bàn fǎ
植一点儿公道都没有，但是他想不出其它的办法。

At the same time, Cao Zhi felt deeply hurt.
This challenge was baseless, but he didn't have
any other solution.

tā kāishǐ yìbiān zǒu yìbiān xiǎng　　tā měi zǒu yī bù　　tā jiù juéde yuè jǐnzhāng
他开始一边走一边想。他每走一步，他就觉得越紧张。

tóngshí　　cáo pī yě shīqù liǎoliǎo nàixīn
同时，曹丕也失去了了耐心。

He began to step and think. For each step he took, he began to feel more and more nervous. Meanwhile, Cao Pi grew more and more impatient.

zǒu dào le dì qī bù yǐ hòu　　cáo zhí ān jìng zhàn zhe bù dòng

走到了第七步以后，曹植安静站着不动。

By the time he took the seventh step, Cao Zhi
stood quietly and did not move.

_{cáo pī bù nài fán dì jiào}　　　_{nǐ yǐ jīng zǒu wán liǎo qī bù}　　_{nǐ de shī ne}
曹丕不耐烦地叫，"你已经走完了七步，你的诗呢？
_{xiǎng bù chū lái ba}
想不出来吧？"

Cao Pi impatiently yelled, "Alright, you've walked your seven steps! Have you thought of a poem?"

cáo zhí kàn le tā gē gē yī yǎn màn màn dì niàn chū tā de shī

曹植看了他哥哥一眼，慢慢地念出他的诗。

Cao Zhi looked his brother in his eye, and slowly he spoke.

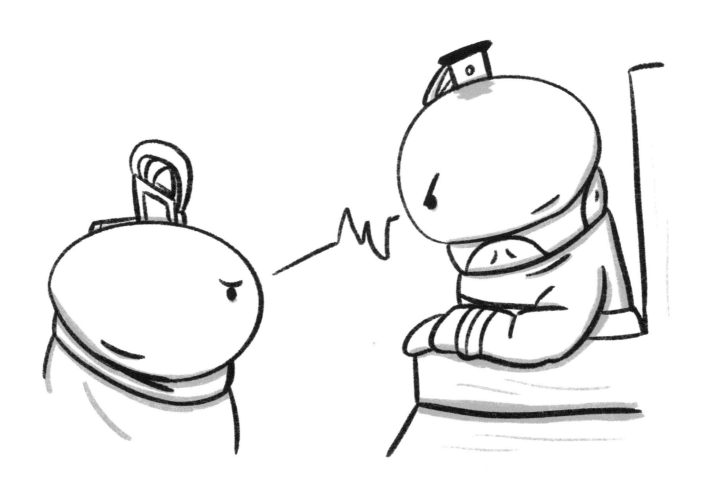

zhǔ dòu rán dòu qí
"煮豆燃豆萁，
dòu zài fǔ zhōng qì
豆在釜中泣，
běn shì tóng gēn shēng
本是同根生，
xiāng jiān hé tài jí
相煎何太急。"

"Beanstalks are ignited to boil beans,
In the pot the beans weep.
Originally they were born from the same root,
Why is it so urgent to fry them?"

dà jiā yī tīng wán cáo zhí de shī quán dōu ān jìng le xià lái
大家一听完曹植的诗，全都安静了下来。

Once he finished, everybody stood in silence.

cáo pī tīng dǒng le cáo zhí shī hòu de yǐn yù mò mò bù shuō huà
曹丕听懂了曹植诗后的隐喻默默不说话。

Cao Pi realized that Cao Zhi had used metaphors, and stopped speaking.

zhèxiē dòu běn shì cóng tónggēn shēng dànshì zài guō xià zhǔ dòu shì dòu qí
这些豆"本是从同根生",但是在锅下煮豆是豆萁。

tāmen de guānxì jiù xiàng cáo zhí yǔ cáo pī xiàn zài de qíngkuàng gē gē xiǎng hài dì dì
它们的关系就像曹植与曹丕现在的情况，哥哥想害弟弟。

Although the beans were from the same pods, the beanstalks were burning the beans. Their relationship was just like Cao Zhi's and Cao Pi's, the older brother wanted to hurt the little brother.

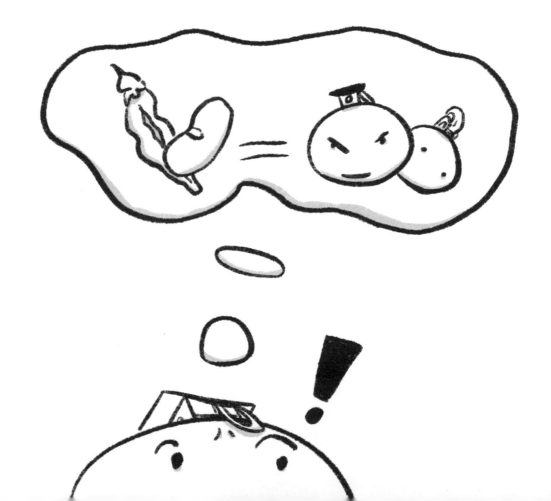

^{cáo pī dǒng le cáo zhí de zhè shǒu hǎo shī hòu tā jiù juéde jīngyà}
曹丕懂了曹植的这首好诗后，他就觉得惊讶；
^{zhè yěshì tā yǒushēngyǐlái dìyī cì gǎndào yǒuxiē cánkuì}
这也是他有生以来第一次感到有些惭愧。

When Cao Pi understood the meaning of Cao Zhi's poem, he felt astonished; this was also the first time in his life that he felt ashamed.

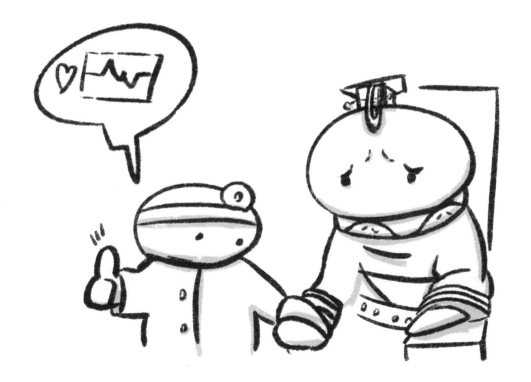

cóngcǐyǐhòu　　cáo pī jiù búzài chùchù zhǎo jīhuì shānghài cáo zhí
从此以后，曹丕就不再处处找机会伤害曹植，

érqiě tā xīnli kāishǐ biànde yuèláiyuè shànliáng
而且他心里开始变得越来越善良。

From this moment onward, Cao Pi did not search
for a way to harm Cao Zhi, and he slowly
became more positive.

háizi men yǒude shíhòu nǐ shìbushì juéde bàba māmā duì nǐ xiōngdì huòzhě
孩子们，有的时候，你是不是觉得爸爸妈妈对你兄弟或者

jiěmèi bǐjiào hǎo nǐ yǒu shénme gǎnjué nǐ huìbuhuì gēn cáo pī yíyàng xiǎngzhǎo
姐妹比较好？你有什么感觉？你会不会跟曹丕一样，想找

yígè jīhuì hài tāmen rúguǒ nǐ zhīdào nǐ xiōngdì huòzhě jiěmèi jídù nǐ nǐ huì
一个机会害他们？如果你知道你兄弟或者姐妹嫉妒你，你会

gēn cáo zhí yíyàng yòng shī lái biǎo dá nǐ de gǎn qíng ma
跟曹植一样用诗来表达你的感情吗？

Children, do you ever feel that your dad and mom like your sibling
more? What would you do? Would you be like Cao Pi, and try to find
some way to hurt them? If you knew that your sibling was jealous of
you, would you be like Cao Zhi and use a poem to express your feelings?

ABOUT THE AUTHOR

Wyatt was born in California. He lives with his mom and dad, two little brothers, and their small dog. He likes to talk with his friends, draw, and relax. He hates brussels sprouts. He hopes to use his translations and artwork to introduce unknown cultural stories to readers.

Printed in the USA
CPSIA information can be obtained
at www.ICGtesting.com
LVHW072314100924

790709LV00001B/1

* 9 7 9 8 8 8 6 7 9 4 8 2 3 *